I0806043

Rob has done the Kingdom a service to bring through this manuscript a clear and concise unveiling of mission that will surprise and challenge you to get a glimpse of God's heart and the Church's calling to the cities of the world. Every leader should read this book and recognize God's mandate for this moment in history.

—Alan Platt
Global Leader, Doxa Deo/City Changers Movement

In Rob Hoskins' *Theology of the City* we're offered something unique within the growing body of literature around Gospel City Movements: a succinct yet rich description and analysis of the impact united, holistic, sustainable movements of churches can have on the places God has planted them.

He's done a great job providing a historical analysis, a biblical basis, and an inspiring call for all who name the name of Jesus to take their part in this fresh effort to embody and declare the present reality of the Kingdom: God's rule and reign in the here and now.

Rob knows what he's writing about. He's a practitioner, having helped found Church United, South Florida's growing GCM. It's only by sharing ideas and resources that we can all continue to see the progress we desperately need, amidst the often chaotic and challenging season we're in.

—Kevin Palau
President and CEO, Luis Palau Association

Cities are the essential place where people have motivation to come together and solve problems. Rob Hoskins has done an awesome job addressing this opportunity and the opportunity that we all have to bring our energies and resources to make lasting change. A must-read for leaders that really want to make a difference.

—Scott Beck
Cofounder and CEO, Gloo

Theology of the City is a masterful, short but densely packed sprint through the vision, biblical framework, recent history, and current inspiration of God's work in global cities. It is an essential first-read for anyone wanting to see a well-prepared map before diving into this fast-growing global movement. It is an insightful synthesis of the core principles of city movements to give helpful anchors of understanding for those who have led citywide unity for decades. Cities are a unique place of opportunity for evangelism, disciple making, Kingdom influence, and joy in experiencing God's delight. Rob Hoskins has captured this opportunity with personal application and vision to open up doors for all of us to see our own cities in new, inspiring ways.

—Brad Smith
Chancellor, Bakke Graduate University

Rob Hoskins has provided a great primer on the theology, history, and analysis of City Gospel Movements. God uniting the church in cities is the story of the Gospel growing in the twenty-first century.

—Mac Pier
Founder of Movement.org

As more and more Christian leaders are sensing a call to play a deeper role in the holistic flourishing of every person in their cities, Rob provides a theological stepping-stone into this great work.

—Eric Swanson
Coauthor, *To Transform a City: Whole Church, Whole Gospel, Whole City*

Rob Hoskins is both a trailblazer and a catalyst. This book will help you not only build a church but also bless a city to the third and fourth generations. It will challenge you to dream bigger, pray harder, and think longer.

—Mark Batterson
New York Times Best-Selling Author, *The Circle Maker*

Theology of the City echoes the call Jesus gave His followers to be "the light of the world" and "a city set on a hill" (Matt. 5:14, NASB). Drawing on his passionate faith, his insight into Scripture, and his expertise as a global development leader, Rob Hoskins informs, inspires, and equips us to share the good news of the Gospel in our increasingly urban world. This book is a must-read for anyone who wants to advance God's Kingdom in diverse and densely populated cities.

—Chris Hodges
Founding Pastor, Church of the Highlands; Author, *Out of the Cave* and *Pray First*

Theology of the City is a must-read for every believer passionate about God's mission for the world. Rob Hoskins provides a compelling biblical perspective on the significance of cities in God's redemptive plan. This thought-provoking work challenges Christians to embrace their calling to seek shalom in the midst of modern-day Babylon. With practical insights and theological depth, *Theology of the City* inspires action and offers hope for Gospel-centered transformation as we labor to advance the city of God in the midst of the city of man. Hoskins' keen cultural analysis grounded in biblical truth is a timely call to the church in the twenty-first century.

—Robert J. Pacienza
Senior Pastor, Coral Ridge Presbyterian Church
Fort Lauderdale, Florida

In *Theology of the City*, Rob Hoskins issues a profound and timely challenge for Christians to reimagine their missional relationship with the urban world. Amid the greatest wave of urban growth in history, this compelling and transformative call to action urges Jesus followers to embrace their role as salt and light in the cities God loves. With theological depth, passion, and practical wisdom, Rob inspires Christians to live with missional purpose and intentionality. Whether you live in a city or not, this concise and powerful book is a must-read that will reshape how you see the world and live out your faith.

—Craig Groeschel
Senior Pastor, Life.Church

THEOLOGY *of the* CITY

ROB HOSKINS

OneHope
600 SW 3rd Street
Pompano Beach, FL 33060
info@onehope.net

ISBN 13: TP: 979-8-9929376-6-4
25 26 27 28 29 — 987654321
Printed in the United States of America

A LETTER TO THE READER

Several years ago, when my younger daughter, Natasha, was seventeen, she approached her mother and me about moving away from home to New York City. A mixture of emotions washed over us. We were thrilled she was seizing this opportunity to pursue her dream, but we were also concerned about the complex realities she would face in her new home in the city.

While we were confronting this new reality at home in our family's journey, I was also facing similar challenges in my ministry life. The global Church was reeling under the weight of urban challenges. In China, the urban house church movement, primarily a rural phenomenon, was losing its youth as a consequence of the greatest forced migration in human history from a rural agrarian to an urban manufacturing economy. In India, extended families were being ripped apart by the emergence of tech metropolis, eroding long-held traditional values.

These personal and professional realities began to consume more and more of my prayer and thought life.

This journey of learning continues today as my family and the world continue their inevitable moment toward a climactic urban future. My theology and passion have had to expand and adapt to what I have learned and have yet to fully understand.

As Natasha attended The New School in New York, she was confronted with questions that I had not prepared her for and I had never had to answer for myself. I had to develop, for her sake and for the sake of global Church partners raising their own youth, a robust theology of the city.

Since I initially crafted this material as part of my doctoral thesis, it warms my heart to see that there is now a growing interest in the theology of the city. I want to clarify that this is not a comprehensive theological treatise on the city; instead, it's a digest, an introduction to this critical field of study. If you desire a deeper exploration of this theology, I highly recommend articles like Timothy Keller's "The Meaning of the City," and more recently, the Bible Project has produced invaluable materials that encourage people to delve deeper into this topic.

This book represents my personal journey in developing my own theology of the city. Here, I share some of my thoughts and experiences surrounding this subject. I firmly believe that every individual should have a theology of the city, and this book marks the beginning of my exploration. I am still on this journey, and I implore all of us to embark on it together, as it's a lifelong endeavor.

This book is designed to be a concise, practical, and accessible overview of my theology of the city. The intention is to make this material approachable and easy to grasp. I also wanted to incorporate the voices of some of my friends in this journey, which is why I invited incredible ministry leaders from megacities around the world to share their insights and firsthand experience.

This book serves as a reflection of the significance of cities in the Bible and how that relates to our modern lives. It's for my daughters and every believer. Whether you currently live in a city or not, we're in the midst of the greatest urban growth in human history. We can't afford to miss this as Christ's body. I invite you to dive into how this reality relates to your own life and ministry.

THEOLOGY OF THE CITY

Engaging in Concentric Circles of Community

Whether at a global, national, local, or personal level, we are responsible to serve the Kingdom and engage with our concentric circles of community and missional praxis. The Lord's demands on my life to ensure that "all things are being made new" has found expression in my personal life throughout these circles. None of the circles are more important than the others, for we must learn to engage with them all in a healthy way. How I act and respond within each sphere is unique.

In the global sense, my calling is more specialized and specific, but as my calling becomes more localized, it becomes more holistic, encompassing more and more of the complete calling of a Christ follower. As I draw closer to my city, I am forced to ask, "What are my roles and responsibilities to make all things new here right now?" This calling grows more expansive as my concentric circle of proximity gets tighter. What am I to my neighbors? Those who live right next door to me? Am I all things to all people, that I might lead some to Christ? Yes, I must endeavor to be everything to them in Christ Jesus. I must seek to live incarnationally. Incarnation embodies everything about who I am, how I act and think. My completeness, my most genuine self must be expressed most acutely in my home—for my wife, children, parents, and grandparents. I have realized that my most genuine, authentic self expressed in the most localized context does not compete with my neighbor, city, regional, national, or global expression of my expanding, less holistic, more specialized calling and action. It enhances and improves it.

My prayer for all of us, as followers of Jesus, is that we renew our commitment to the places where God has called us and that we become more fully engaged with the hope and future He has for these cities that are yearning for the salt and light of the Gospel that we have been so freely given by Jesus our Lord.

Why Do We Need a Theology of the City?

Every season of human history has its sociocultural challenges. As humanity's tide flows into the world's cities at exponential rates, God is on the move, and He welcomes His people into joining others in pursuing His mission. Having unity of mission in reaching our cities is essential to the unfolding of the *missio Dei*, the mission of God.

Missiology[1] does not exist in a vacuum. It is a living, breathing movement in response to the sociological challenges and opportunities our culture and context presents. The challenges we are facing when it comes to the twenty-first-century city are perhaps more daunting, complex, and spiritually powerful than any frontier we have yet encountered. We must remember that Jesus' final appeal to His disciples was for unity. Jesus prayed "that all of them may be one, Father, just as you are in me and I am in you. May they also be in us so that the world may believe that you have sent me" (John 17:21). If Jesus' final appeal was for unity among His disciples, we cannot afford to ignore this unity mandate today.

To this end, we must labor together to be salt and light in our cities of the world so that we become a living witness of the city of God.

Another important concept includes the emergence of Gospel City Movements (GCMs), which appear to be a natural response to the challenges that the Church of our day faces. A GCM, a concept we will be further exploring in this book, is a united, holistic, sustainable effort by the citywide Church to seek the peace and prosperity of their city. It's crucial to understand that this concept falls on a continuum that is constantly growing and being refined, so you may have heard similar terms used to describe it, such as Transformational City Network. However, for clarity's sake, we will be using the above definition throughout this book.

Expanding GCMs is a manifest expression of Jesus' prayer for unity and mission being fulfilled in our day. By understanding GCMs' shared identity and advancing how they are organized, we can further partner for the purpose of spreading God's Kingdom on earth as it is in heaven.

I am passionate about GCMs because I see them as a move of God that is desperately needed for such a time as this. This conviction led me to focus my doctoral research and dissertation[2] on learning more about GCMs, including what constitutes their core identity and how they might be organized for greatest effectiveness. The research included in-depth interviews with the executive leaders of seven prominent GCMs in the United States. This book is a distillation of several key findings that came out of my doctoral research. The emerging results are framed using the voice of the participants themselves, which are identified with quotations to honor their anonymity.

We will explore how to best engage with cities in the twenty-first century from several important lenses, including sociological, biblical, historical, and contemporary perspectives. These vistas provide a foundation for a more robust understanding of how we as followers of Christ can develop our core identity to serve our cities and help churches not just survive but thrive. I'll briefly touch on the science of collective impact (CI) because it holds great potential to inform and enhance the operational effectiveness of the Church in our present reality.

Trends Shaping Today's Cities

The world is becoming increasingly urban. According to the Population Reference Bureau, in 1900, only 14 percent of the world's population lived in urban areas; by 1950, this number grew to 30 percent.[3] In 2008, a tipping point occurred when the world became 51 percent urban.[4] By 2050, it is estimated that the world population will be nearly 70 percent urban.[5]

The reality of urbanization[6] has generated tremendous missiological implications. An entire field of urban missiology has started to build around the fresh cry that "the greatest need of our day is for the Gospel to enliven first our hearts, and then, our cities."[7]

Modern Urbanization

Globalization and modern urbanization[8] are creating unique challenges and opportunities for our current missiological realities. As our sociological dynamics shift, we are seeing unprecedented religious and cultural diversity flow into our cities. The late urban leader Ray Bakke put it this way:

By 2050,it is estimated that the world population will be nearly 70 percent urban.

> As we move away from a world of nations to a world of interconnected multinational cities, it's clear that the frontier of mission has shifted. The majority of the world's non-Christians will not be geographically distant peoples, but culturally distant peoples who often reside together within the shadows of urban spires in the metro areas of every continent.[9]

The social trends of urbanization and globalization have also amplified pluralism[10] in the city. As people with widely diverse cultures, beliefs, and religious commitments live in closer and closer proximity, tolerance and public secularism are increasing.

The Church in the City

Because we are experiencing increasingly urbanized, globalized, pluralistic cities, the need for a unified witness of the Gospel has become even more critical. As the Church engages in theological reflection and refreshes its practices, we will see a strong, emerging trend toward organizing sustainable collaboration by local church leaders for joint missional expression.

Current sociological pressures are forcing local churches to consider new levels of cooperation with other local churches that hold similar basic theological and missiological perspectives in order to contend with these realities.

Timothy Keller observes, "What it takes to reach a city is a city-wide gospel movement."[11] He explains that a Gospel "movement needs the dynamic of cooperation that encourages people of different temperaments and perspectives to come together around their common vision and goals."[12]

A Biblical Perspective of the City

In an increasingly urban world, the Church needs to reconnect with the theological significance that the Bible places on the nature and role of the city in God's unfolding story. While the Scriptures reveal cities as irrevocably tied to the eternal plans of God, today "most Christians still read the Bible through rural lenses."[13] Robert Linthicum explains:

> We enter the city equipped with an urban sociology and urban tools for ministry, but we carry with us the baggage of a theology designed in rural Europe. Even the very way we formulate theological questions and the frameworks we use to construct our theological thought have been forged from our rural past. What we are in need of is a theology as urban as our sociology and missiology.[14]

The Bible's theological portrait of the city includes its nature, role, and characteristics, along with God's disposition, plan, and missionary calling toward it. At least five significant developments progressively unfold throughout the metanarrative of Scripture: (1) the creation of the first city, (2) God's response to the city, (3) Jesus and the city, (4) the Church and the city, and (5) the final chapter of the city.

The Creation of the First City

The creation of the first city began when Cain attempted to defy God by building a city as a symbol of self-protection and identity apart from Him.

In the Genesis narrative, we see sin deviously festered in the original family then graphically portrayed when Cain murdered his brother, Abel. God's subsequent judgment upon Cain called for him to become a "fugitive" and a "wanderer" in the world (Gen. 4:12, NKJV, NIV). God promised to protect Cain, but Cain rejected God's protection. "So Cain went out from the LORD's presence and...was then building a city" (Gen. 4:16–17). He calls the city Enoch. The word means initiation. Always starting, never satisfied, he is going to start a new world. Unlike Eden, created in God's nature, he will manufacture his own creation.

This pattern of rebellion was further perpetuated by Nimrod, "a mighty hunter before the LORD" (Gen. 10:9), and his proliferation of other early cities in Genesis. While Nimrod went on to build the ancient cities of Nineveh, Calah, and Resen, the center of his kingdom was Babylon, "the gate of the gods," which became "the place of confusion."[15]

Babylon was the megacity of its day. Its emphasis was on independence, resisting God's commands, and extending separation from God. As Keller explains, "The spirit of the line of Cain reaches its climax in this effort to build the city of [Babylon]. The new city and its tower are designed to help residents gain an identity apart from the service of God."[16] Babylon was the early example of the city as a prideful expression of resisting God and seeking identity apart from Him. When God saw Babylon's self-destructive plan underway, He intervened for the protection of His own creation and plan of redemption. God continues to respond to the rebelliousness of the city throughout history and to this day with a compassionate, redemptive disposition, plan, and missionary calling.

God's Response to the City

God's response to the city is highlighted in the stories of Sodom, Jonah and Nineveh, and the Babylonian captivity. The books of Isaiah, Psalms, and Ezekiel also highlight

God's merciful response to the city continues, expressed by His willingness to relent from wrath and save cities where His people are present.

contrasts between the city of God and the city of man. In the story of Sodom (Gen. 18–19), God's merciful response to the city continues, expressed by His willingness to relent from wrath and save cities where His people are present (Gen. 18:32; Jer. 5:1). God's response to the city involves using His people and their presence to bear influence within the city and bring others to Himself.

The story of Jonah and Nineveh further demonstrates God's redemptive disposition and important regard for the city, as Jonah, the reluctant missionary, is called to bring God's message to the city. Several times in the story of Jonah, Nineveh is described as a "great city" (Jon. 1:2; 3:2–3; 4:11), indicating a special importance to its size and influence.

Nineveh was a city of strategic missionary import because more of God's creation was concentrated there in one place, and the city itself possessed privileged influence at that particular moment of history. The missionary response of God to the city of Nineveh (Jon. 4:11) is not an isolated story of His love to one city, but it is rather a declaration consistent with His purpose and missional strategy toward all cities. Jonah's task is our task: to fulfill a permanent and pervading missionary calling to God's people until His final Kingdom and glorious new city has come.

From the context of the Babylonian captivity, Jeremiah 29:4–14 emerges as a continuing framework for how God's people of all time are called to respond to the context of whatever city in which they live. James Davison Hunter used this passage in developing his theology of faithful presence to point out that exile didn't mean abandonment, but rather indicated the place and context in which God was at work:

> Exile did not mean that God had abandoned Israel. Rather, exile was the place where God was at work. God's purposes with Israel, in other

> words, were served by the Babylonian invasion. God, as the text repeats, "sent" them into exile.... Exile would clearly last long beyond the present generation....Clearly it would have been justifiable for the Jews to be hostile to their captors. It also would have been natural enough for them to withdraw from engaging the world around them. By the same token, it would have been easy for them to simply assimilate with the culture that surrounded them. Any of these three options made sense in human terms. But God was calling them to something different—not to be defensive against, isolated from, or absorbed into the dominant culture, but to be faithfully present within it.[17]

The Babylonian captivity demonstrates that the city, although often a place of evil, is at the same time being used by God as an instrument of mission to draw the nations to Himself. As Keller describes, "While living in Babylon, they are not simply to increase their tribe in a ghetto within the city; they are to use their resources to benefit the common good."[18] God calls us to faithfully engage in the city for its good without being assimilated by it or becoming isolated within it.

The Old Testament books of Isaiah, Psalms, and Ezekiel highlight the city of God as a counter-cultural and sociological vision that is set in contrast to the sinful inclinations that symbolize the city of man (Isa. 26:1–4). Jerusalem is the archetypical city that God established in the Old Testament. Keller believes that "the biggest change in the city's role within redemptive history comes with the establishment of Jerusalem" and that it was "appointed to be an urban culture that is a witness to the nations and a symbol of the future City of God."[19] Daniel and his mentorship of Israelite youths is a powerful illustration of living with a hope and a future under the rule and reign of God. They were exiles living with purpose and significance in the heart of the most powerful city in the world, understanding their times and knowing the ways of the Babylonians better than the Babylonians, but knowing when not to eat the king's meat. They were living in the tension of the city between bowing and praying to the King of kings, honoring and serving the common good of the civic and political power, but never bending the knee and bowing under the pressure to the point of suffering and persecution. God's presence and joy constitute the city of God (Ps. 48:1–3), whose prophetic promise is for all of humanity as a future mixed-race city (see Ezek. 16:60–63). The future city of God constitutes the rest, blessing, and shalom of human life in its most exalted state. (See Revelation 21–22.) This future city of God will be the ultimate fulfillment of the perpetual presence and peace of God. The strong city of God provides peace for all its inhabitants, in contrast to the city of man, which is marked by pride, selfishness, insecurity, and sin.

Jesus and the City

The coming and work of Christ further illuminates a biblical perspective of the city. As Jacques Ellul explained, "Thus the history of the city, divided in two by Jesus Christ, goes from Eden to Jerusalem, from a garden to a city. God created man in a garden, in the middle of the world."[20] It's not by accident that the climax of Jesus' story will be in the city of Jerusalem.

Alvin Padilla further explains:

> Jesus clearly embraced the idea of the importance of the city for the proclamation of the advent of the Kingdom of God. His central message is that the promises of God have begun to be fulfilled

> in His own person. He has arrived on the scene as the divine King ready to reclaim, redirect, and redeem His people. To the cities, Jesus sends His disciples with a message: the Kingdom of God is at hand.[21]

The timing of Jesus' arrival was in step with a new Roman urbanization. At the outset of His ministry, the devil tempted Jesus by offering Him the cities of the world (Matt. 4:8–10). However, Jesus' full victory at the cross, the resurrection, and His second coming will usher in a far better Kingdom than Satan and this world could ever offer. As the Son of man had "no place to lay his head" (Luke 9:58), Jesus bore the curse of Cain and all of humanity. As Ellul explained:

> Cain wanted nothing to do with his sentence. Cain revolted and built the city. It was against man's will that he was nevertheless a wanderer on the face of the earth, broken away from his environment. But Jesus took the full condition of man. Totally man, except for sin. But that means that he had to accept the consequences of sin.... The God of heaven is a wanderer. He has taken Cain's curse upon himself. Jesus will take the mark of Cain upon himself; he is willing to live a life fully under God's protection with no fear for shelter in a home built by man. The city is not his home, it is a place to proclaim the Kingdom of God.[22]

Jesus replaces Jerusalem as the "place" for all believers of all time, so that "the coming of Jesus significantly changed the status of Jerusalem and that Jesus himself claimed to be 'greater than the temple' (Matthew 12:6),"[23] as John Inge points out:

> Among New Testament authors there is a clear consensus that Jesus is the new temple that the

> genuine mercy seat, the true place of God's presence, is no longer the Ark of the Covenant, but Christ crucified. God was in Christ reconciling the world to himself (2 Corinthians 5:19), and as such Christ not only brought the temple system to a close, he is himself the spiritual temple, the new dwelling place of God.[24]

Jesus also replaces civic leaders and Caesar as the new King. The word *Gospel* normally carried political reference. The coins of the Roman empire referred to Caesar as "Son of God" and "Savior of the World," so the Gospel writers are very explicitly framing Jesus as the new King of the world, greater than Caesar or any human authority.

The Church and the City

Central to the development of the Church and the city are an urban strategy and an urban lifestyle. The Book of Acts reveals a prevailing urban strategy that resulted in the rapid expansion of God's Kingdom. The noun *city* (Greek *polis*) is used 160 times in the New Testament with about half of these usages found in Luke and Acts.[25] The focus on the city is so paramount throughout the Book of Acts that "it is no exaggeration to say that the book of Acts deals almost entirely with cities; missionary work is almost limited to them."[26] In *The First Urban Christians*, Wayne Meeks therefore argues that Pauline Christianity "was entirely urban....The village culture of Palestine had been left behind, and the Greco-Roman city became the dominant environment of the Christian movement."[27]

A city-focused strategy is significant because cities are centrally situated and possess a unique power for social influence. If the Gospel is "unfolded at the urban center, you can effectively reach the region and the surrounding society."[28] Paul also intentionally leveraged the potential of cities:

> St. Paul's centres were centres indeed. He seized strategic points because he had a strategy. The foundation of churches in them was part of a campaign. In his hands they became the sources of rivers, mints from which the new coin of the Gospel was spread in every direction. They were centres from which he could start new work with new power. But they were this not only because they were naturally fitted for this purpose, but because his method of work was so designed that centres of intellectual and commercial activity became centres of Christian activity.[29]

For Paul, cities became representatives of the entire world.[30] It was in the planting and growing of churches in cities that Paul envisioned "the formation of new urban communities created and loved by God."[31]

The New Testament focus on urban strategy pays close attention to an urban lifestyle. At the center of this urban lifestyle are the virtues of faith, hope, and love (1 Cor. 13:12–13). The cohesive nature of these core qualities is ascribed to the Christian lifestyle as values to live by in the temporary cities of our day that will be fully realized in the city of God to come.

- Faith is central to an urban lifestyle because the Church is called to see and interpret meaning in the world in such a way that it provides compelling reasons for the truth of Christ and a vision for the way of life in Christ. This requires a "thick Gospel," a healthy catechesis for us to build a construct for truth in an environment of many truths. "The witness of the church has always taken place within a pluralistic milieu. During recent years, however,

We are called to sacrifice our own ambition to make known the name above all names, the name of Jesus.

new perceptions of this milieu have emerged, and pluralism is fast assuming the character of an ideology."[32] A thin Gospel cannot respond to the challenges of this emerging urban pluralism. Faith must be grounded in timeless and biblical truth and applied in relevant dynamic ways if the Church is going to have a meaningful community and voice.

- Truth expressed by effectively answering the questions that a pluralistic, postmodern, relativistic city is asking its citizens must be at the heart and core of a biblical theology embedded into our preaching, evangelism, discipleship, and church-planting content and strategies.
- The advent of the digital age and its accompanying superpowers is creating a hyperbolic explosion of connectivity and ubiquitous knowledge that is building a new tower to the heavens; "the singularity" describes the hypothetical point at which technology—in particular artificial intelligence (AI) powered by machine learning algorithms—reaches a superhuman level of intelligence and capability. Instead of making the Church more irrelevant, it should awaken us to a greater need the city will have, not for knowledge (*gnosis*), which will become cheaper and cheaper, but understanding (*synesis*), which will become more valuable, and wisdom (*sophia*), which will become invaluable for humanity's survival. Paul lays this out to the Church of Colossae in chapter 1 verses 9–10: "So we have not stopped praying for you since we first heard about you. We ask God to give you complete knowledge [*gnosis*] of his will and to give you spiritual wisdom [*sophia*] and understanding [*synesis*]. Then the way you live will always honor and please the Lord, and your lives will produce every kind of good fruit. All the while, you will grow as you learn to know God

better and better." Our truth from the Scripture and our divine wisdom, coming down from the Father through the supernatural power of the Holy Spirit, are essential for the cities of our world.

- Hope and a theology of purposeful work are essential—a calling into every sphere of the cities' life: business as mission, art as mission, education as mission, every expression of city civic life expressed through a personal calling and an ecclesial business model that uses the property, talent, and resources of the Church as a gift and a useful common good. Urban city planners actually have a technical name for churches: locally unwanted land uses (LULUs). They see them as providing no tax revenue and no civic or commercial value to the city. Why would they want churches when a church building is utilized only 17 percent of an average workweek instead of being fully maximized as a business, nonprofit, or educational institution?
- The virtue of love is the central and greatest testimony of the Gospel. The Church is called to embody and express God's love in service for the good of the city, as it lives incarnationally within the city. Community is an antidote to the loneliness and isolation of city life. A community so filled with love for one another and in service to their neighbors is the strongest witness the Church has ever had. As Lesslie Newbigin says, "The only effective hermeneutic of the Gospel is the life of the congregation which believes it."[33] Jesus' loving Gospel is portrayed by a healthy, authentic, and loving community.

The Final Chapter of the City

In the final chapter of the city, the city of God comes as an expanded fulfillment of God's original creation in the Garden of Eden, a future garden city (Rev. 21–22). The coming of the city of God will include the final contrast between Babylon as the city of man and God's perfect city filled with peace and productivity. Here, the desires of humanity will one day be fully realized by God's people.

In light of God's coming prophetic city in the final chapter of His story, we might be tempted to ask ourselves: "Why build, invest, or work at all? If it is entirely God's work, His new creation, are we not made obsolete and should we not disengage from any participation in the city of man?" Keller answers this objection by explaining that "Revelation shows us this is not the case. God's intention for human endeavor is that it raise up civilizations—cities—that glorify him and steward the endless wonders and riches that God put into the created world."[34]

The final city of God will fulfill the desires of human existence by providing a lasting satisfaction of *roots*, *place*, and *destination*.[35]

- Roots speak to beliefs and faith.
- Place speaks to belonging and love.
- Destination speaks to purpose and hope.

The vision of God for the city, wrapped in faith, hope, and love, is God's gift to His people. What Cain built in rebellion at the beginning in the city of man, God will one day redeem in love at the end—in the city of God.

The History of the Church and the City Matters

As a living system, the Church has always existed in constantly changing historical forms.[36] From the New Testament, we see a "multiplicity of different types of Churches" that arose with unique strengths and weaknesses, diverse theological challenges, and distinctive cultural particularities and personalities.[37] Nevertheless, although the early Church developed cultural groupings, worship styles, and leadership affinities, on the whole they still maintained a central ethos of "one church of the City" with multiple congregations.[38]

The Epistles were often addressed to cities because cities were the normal ecclesiastical unit of measurement (Romans, Ephesians, Philippians, Colossians, Galatians). These cities had multiple house churches, yet Paul would address them as believers in the city, not as separate entities.

Throughout Church history we see that relatedness between church communities informs how the Church expresses itself. Since its earliest beginnings, the Church has been forming, splintering, reforming, and experiencing different movements of renewal and revitalization. Through councils, revivals, and reformations, the Church has constantly sought to understand and operate in light of who the Church is and how it relates to itself and to an ever-changing world.

More recently, urbanization, globalization, digitalization, and pluralism have shaped the emerging trends creating rich soil for the Church to grow and serve God's creation at this time in history.

City Spotlight: Heart of God Church Singapore

Singapore, Dubai, and Miami are unique global destinations. Miami is where North America meets South America; Dubai is where the North meets the South; and Singapore is where the East meets the West. These have become major capitals of finance and fun, where neighboring nations have a place to play together as well as parking massive financial fortunes. These are also spots where people from more restrictive communities can come and do things they might not be able to do in their own countries. Singapore, Dubai, and Miami have become examples of pluralistic city-states that, in some ways, are more powerful than entire nations.

Two leaders who have modeled what it means to build a great church in one of these complex city spaces are Tan Seow How (Pastor How) and his wife, Cecilia Chan (Pastor Lia). They are the founding senior pastors of Heart of God Church in Singapore, which has more than four thousand members. One of the church's most impressive aspects is that the average age of its members is twenty-three. This unique model has allowed young people to contribute to every aspect of the church services and church growth.

So, how in the world can someone plant and grow a church in a pluralistic environment primarily through young people?

"How it happened was God challenged us: build a church for youth by youth to reach youth, and we just obeyed God." —Pastor How

In 1999, Pastor How was leading a church with about forty adults when Pastor Lia felt God telling her to raise up the foundations of many generations. She went ahead and began discipling nine teenagers from the children's church. Soon, her youth group had a revival and Pastors How and Lia shifted their focus to plant the church through young people, empowering them in every kind of responsibility. Today, it has grown into the thousands of young people they have in their church today.

This is amazing for many reasons, one being that you almost never hear of someone planting a church with children and young people. In fact, not even How recommends it unless God calls you to it. Most people are resistant to focusing on children and youth first because adults have the influence and power in society. Most church planters believe they have to start with the people of influence who can tithe and pay the bills. This is especially true for Singapore, which is currently considered the most expensive city in the world to live in.

However, it has been twenty-plus years since Lia had the original vision, and now Heart of God is a powerful church with thousands of young people. Attendees feel its energy and vibrancy, but it's not just because it's a bunch of young people; it's because it begins to feel like home. There is an incredible sense of unity, belonging, and community among its members.

"When you focus on making your church a spiritual home for the next generation, young people will build it, fight for it, and sacrifice for it." —Pastor How

Pastors How and Lia knew that though the youth in Singapore might have legal families, in some ways, they're orphans in the city. As we see in the Bible, the city is a powerful force; it demands things of you. Due to the cost of living and surviving in a place like Singapore, many kids give up their childhood as they're left alone while both of their parents work. I love how these pastors have made Heart of God more than a church that people attend on

Sunday but a family instilling hope in kids who perhaps have lost hope in their own families.

Making Heart of God Church feel like a home for the youth in Singapore did not happen by accident. The couple transformed the way the church has traditionally made disciples. Usually, churches want a person to believe first, then they belong, and then they become a disciple of others. How and Lia saw that the young people of their city needed something different—their need to belong was too great. At the Heart of God Church, young people *belong* first. Making this change has transformed the lives of countless youth in Singapore.

"We see that young people, the next generation, need to belong first. Then subsequently, eventually, gradually... then they will believe, and then they will become disciples." —Pastor How

Not only do young people feel like this church is a place of belonging and community, they also feel like it's a place of purpose. Heart of God Church is a living example of an empowered next-gen church. When you go behind the scenes, you'll see young people anywhere from thirteen to twenty years of age working the sound systems and cameras as they direct and produce the service. It's amazing to see how excited they are about serving and leading this way.

"One of our mantras is that youth are not just leaders of tomorrow. Now, obviously, they are the leaders of the future. That is a no-brainer. But they are also leaders today." —Pastor How

With the integration of fresh, young perspectives into the service design, programming, and audio visuals, Heart of God Church remains on the cutting edge of relevant trends that connect with a vibrant audience. Even the architecture of their auditorium, being a stage that extends to the middle of the audience, feels more like a lively concert venue than a traditional church.

How and Lia found a way to give young people in the city belonging and community as well as purpose and empowerment. However, when we go back to when Nimrod founded the city of Babel, it says everyone went there to make a name for themselves (Gen. 11:4). That's the spirit of the city. So, how do Pastors How and Lia instill a Kingdom perspective in their youth to make it clear that though there's nothing wrong with making a name for themselves in Singapore, God has a higher calling for their lives?

First, How and Lia understand what their culture and city demands. In Singapore and many other Asian countries, if you're not excelling in academics, you're not being a dutiful child to your parents. That overarching worldview is so strongly built into the fabric of their culture that their diligence and work ethic are tied to their very character and values. They are in the tension that exists in the city between success, significance, wealth, purpose, identity, and honoring the culture of the family.

Since money and success are what drive the city and nation, How and Lia are very intentional about not preaching a prosperity Gospel. They have noticed many of their young people realize that money cannot buy them happiness, and that's when they point them to Jesus. However, they don't stop at Jesus and salvation. Instead, they focus on teaching about character, vision, purpose, and seeking the Kingdom of God first. This is how they're navigating the city for the next generation.

We, as the Church, have a responsibility to develop a theology of faith, hope, and love for the city. We see this modeled by Jesus as He didn't leave us with just a book;

He left us with a community. He left us with a group of people that He had invested in relationally that trusted Him so much they were able to listen, understand, and continue building the Church. I've found that this generation is so hungry for love and community, but you can't have it without accountability. Pastor How and Pastor Lia have built a community that's so safe, genuine, and authentic (which are values the next generations are hungry for) that they're ready to accept the fact that they're a part of the body of Christ and are accountable to one another. It's not trying to hold accountability from a historical and traditional hierarchy but from a relational community perspective. This is a New Testament model, and it works today.

Pastor How and Pastor Lia truly love the younger generation, and God has given them a special gift to serve and empower them. I am so thankful that they continuously live a theology of faith, hope, and love for their city and are building a model that the rest of the world can see in the Heart of God Church.

Listen to my extended conversation with Pastor How by following the QR code to the video!

The Current State of Gospel City Movements

The early decades of the twentieth century saw a growing fissure between fundamentalism[39] and liberalism.[40] New voices began to emerge and call for a more thoughtful approach to the cultural challenges that were being faced in the middle of the twentieth century. In his contemporary foreword to Carl Henry's classic book *The*

Uneasy Conscience of Modern Fundamentalism, Richard Mouw observes:

> Carl F. H. Henry and others who would soon come to be known as the leaders of a "neo-evangelicalism"[41] were deeply concerned that those Christians known as "fundamentalists" or "evangelicals"[42]—the terms were interchangeable at the time—were ill-equipped to address the crucial issues of the day.[43]

The thinking of Henry and his contemporaries provided a theological perspective and vision that formed the foundational underpinnings of what is needed today. The twentieth century also gave birth to Pentecostalism. African-American, poorer uneducated blue-collar workers, and immigrants living in cities sought out a Pentecostal expression of worship and supernatural expression. During this era, the Azusa Street Revival, and others like it, propelled the Pentecostal movement forward, and it grew so fast that by 1979, 19 percent of all Americans considered themselves Pentecostal or Charismatic, according to a *Christianity Today* Gallup Poll.[44] It was in the context of urban ministry where these fresh perspectives found the most fertile reception.

Ray Bakke, describing the origins of his thinking about urban ministry, found that as a pastor in Chicago he was unprepared for the despair and hopelessness of his people. Bakke expressed that in the mid-1960s for the first time in his life he "saw what an urban church and its pastor could be and do if they combined biblical and theological integrity with contextual engagement of the issues of the day."[45]

The urban reality stands on an extremely complex and nuanced foundation, which demands urban ministry to have a deeper understanding of its history and needs. Bakke was making his observations right at the tail-end of the urban "great migration," which heightened the need for urban ministry. In his thoughtful analysis, Clifford Green tracks the "great migration" that took place from the late 1890s to the 1960s. This time frame consisted of African-Americans moving from the rural south to northern cities. This was a social phenomenon perpetuated by the availability of manufacturing jobs and an attempt to escape the prejudice of rural communities.[46] This resulted in a deeper divide between urban minorities and the wealthier white suburbs, and churches throughout urban areas began to grow and serve within their communities.

The 1950s and 1960s caused a renewed Christian concern for the city as urban minorities filled the cities searching for opportunities. Black churches especially maintained a deep-rooted evangelical orthodoxy, but also committed themselves to the Social Gospel Movement as they sought racial justice for their community. Charles Van Engen details how the Social Gospel Movement and more liberally bent denominations placed a priority on urban ministry, and between 1962 and 1975 established twenty-seven action training centers in twenty-two large U.S. cities to help the church cope with urban social issues.

According to many urban missiologists,[47] "Bakke contributed more than anyone else to create this (present) awareness."[48] Significant themes emerge from his scholarship and practical ministry that are foundational to present expressions, including:

- a commitment to spiritual transformation of persons and social transformation of place,
- a commitment of unity that helps local congregations define their identity and security in the Church universal, and

- a commitment to love neighbors in witness and service.[49]

These foundational expressions of Bakke are similar to Keller's more contemporary vision of urban mission. Keller presents his framework in a theological vision that encompasses these three central elements:

1. Gospel: a central common evangelical orthodoxy that does not tend toward either law or license.
2. City: a balanced contextual cultural approach to present urban realities that neither over nor under adapt the Gospel to its context.
3. Movement: a commitment to work in common cause to reach a city or work for the common good without relinquishing individual church traditions or doctrine.[50]

These three central elements can be seen in Keller's descriptive summary of the composition and goals of GCMs: "Christians and churches coming together across racial and denominational lines in a city, unified by the Gospel and a vision to reach that city." He explains that successful GCMs "see the urban body of Christ grow in quality and quantity faster than the population so that the salt and light of Christian love and truth will actually influence the life of that city, renew it, improving it socially, influencing it culturally and lifting up Jesus' name so it's increasingly respected and honored in that city."[51]

Both Bakke's and Keller's perspectives arose out of their shared contexts in facing the social upheavals of the 1960s and 1970s. During this era, Keller was ministering on a university campus during the Vietnam protest, and he was seeking ways of engaging students in a relevant and dynamic way. Bakke, as a young church planter in Chicago, faced social issues that his traditional white evangelical upbringing could not address. As he recounted, "Nothing prepared me for the cultural captivity and failure of my church under pressure."[52] These two pioneers and thought leaders of the present-day GCM phenomena epitomize the emerging spirit of an evangelical community seeking to reconcile the long-standing fissure that racially and theologically divided the Protestant American church beginning in the latter part of the nineteenth century.

Growing political pragmatism is thwarting these values in the United States and other places as Evangelicals have sought a temporal identity playing to survivalist fears as they see traditional values and norms erode. But again, the answer is not found in opposition or assimilation but in living as a thoughtful witness community of fruitful presence—a light in the midst of darkness, salt in a world losing its flavor.

Although this example has centered on the North American reality, similar tensions face the global Church as it encounters different contextual challenges. The rural mindset of global evangelicalism has fostered a growing awareness across Africa, Asia, and Latin America that new modalities and fresh theology is needed to confront globalization's relentless intrusion of postmodern relativism and pluralism that is eroding traditional and tightly held sociocultural and religious beliefs. I personally have encountered, and continue to serve on every continent, Christian leaders and ministries that are forming new ecclesiastical responses and structures to the emergence of hyper-urbanization. Although contextual responses remain a necessary priority, common thinking and praxis are finding new life in a new "from all to all" missiology that is finding its greatest impetus and collaboration around ministry to the next generation in an urban reality.

City Spotlight: Watoto Church Uganda

When I'm asked for examples of great transformation churches really impacting their cities, I immediately think of my friend Pastor Julius Rwotlonyo from Watoto Church, serving in the heart of Kampala, Uganda.

Even how Watoto Church was established serves as a testament to the kind of unifying and innovative churches we need in cities today. Watoto Church was truly the first of its kind in Kampala when it was started in 1984 by missionaries Gary and Marilyn Skinner.

Up to that point, some churches offered English translation, but Watoto Church fully embraced English, the national language, as a unifying factor of the congregation. Pastor Julius reflects on how that initial decision still influences the dynamic of the congregation of more than thirty-five thousand and multiple locations. Many unifying factors allow people from different tribes to come together and connect in a shared space.

"We all come from different tribes with notable differences in culture. But when we gather as the body of Christ, it's a community of faith. And it's a place where we put aside our tribal differences or social status, and we come united around Christ and the common cause of championing His desires for our city." —Pastor Julius Rwotlonyo

With a diverse blend of people comes tension and challenges too. An urban church is designed to attract many different types of people that represent the whole community. The tension exists between honoring tradition, culture, and individual languages but also feeling like in the midst of a pluralistic city, the church has to accommodate for everyone to feel, in some sense, a new corporate communal identity as Watoto Church and Kingdom people.

Pastor Julius explains that Watoto Church welcomes all kinds of people from all cultures but that all must submit to the truth of God's Word, as it is the final authority.

"There are great things that come from the diversity of cultures, these make them unique and beautiful, for example, food, dressing, dance, and music to mention but a few; it's absolutely phenomenal. But we also realize that there are some bad aspects in our cultures that are based on lies or mystery. So, much as we welcome all people from every culture, we all must submit our cultures to the truth of God's Word. That's the final authority when it comes to matters of truth as well as everyday life." —Pastor Julius Rwotlonyo

The Church acts as Christ's ambassador and, in many cases, ambassadors of reconciliation. People from Watoto Church began to marry people of different tribes, sometimes with backlash from family members outside the church. Watoto Church helped lead those family members in cordial conversations to try and help mend those relationships. In other cases, reconciliation wasn't possible, and Watoto Church continued to be a supportive community for the newlyweds. Watoto Church is a place of love where people feel safe, even when their families reject them.

Some of Watoto Church's greatest ministry opportunities have been to love people even when their families have turned away. It's allowed open doors and conversations for ministry, particularly to Muslim women and families who have been abandoned by their husbands. Love and care for vulnerable communities have resulted in influence among communities who would not ordinarily be open to the Gospel message.

Watoto Church's congregation spans Kampala society, and from the very beginning, they've been intentionally fostering a community that didn't cater to one group over another, whether it was those with more finances or people from a certain political party. They directly focus on communicating that they see themselves as children of God first and foremost. At Watoto Church, their small-group settings are geographical and intentionally integrate people from all walks of life to model how everyone is a valued child of God.

Other challenges they've had to address in their church include the topic of polygamy, practiced throughout pockets of Africa, and Christianity being seen as a Western religion that has no place in Uganda. Watoto Church, standing firm on Scripture, has had to meet the challenge of presenting truth in love in these contexts. As the next generation grapples with these questions and more, other churches and denominations have turned to Watoto Church, asking how they've been able to navigate these conversations with a young generation that is pressing for guidance.

"God's helping us see more success as we continue to do three things that the Apostle Paul says will remain. Faith—not just in words but in visible action; hope—inspire hope for the future not just for individual lives, but hope as well for a great city, continent, and also hope for eternity; love—we preach the message of love and unity when it comes to political, social, or tribal differences." —Pastor Julius Rwotlonyo

People often move into the city hoping for a good job or some level of success, but what people are most looking for is a life of meaning, which walking with Jesus offers. This search for meaning directly relates to Pastor Julius' own story as a teenager. After seeing the Gospel presented in a dynamic artistic-drama format, he realized his life could have a great impact on others, and later when he joined Watoto as a teenager, he saw firsthand that the church existed to make a difference in the city.

Watoto Church is certainly making a difference in their city as a beacon of hope and light! Pastor Julius shared how their church community has been able to minister to people from other religions.

"We realized that some of the needs in our community included the brokenness of especially women who are trying to raise their kids. Very intentionally through our small groups, we started to realize some of those were Muslim women, probably one of many wives who had been left or abandoned. And as a church, our response was to love and practically care for them through our small groups....That love opens a door for us to share the Gospel." —Pastor Julius Rwotlonyo

In addition to the vibrant small groups, the church family cares for more than three thousand motherless and fatherless children twenty-four hours a day, seven days a week. They have one of the largest orphan care programs in Africa. Initially, much of the start-up funding for this program came from the West, but Watoto Church has greatly expanded its capacity to support this work locally.

"A lot of the support was coming from the West. And it was necessary then because it took a lot of investment to get it going. But we are seeing a shift right now where people in the church and Ugandans at large are taking ownership of this work by stepping up to support this work financially." —Pastor Julius Rwotlonyo

This undertaking has been a ten-year journey as more and more congregants have stepped up in generosity to reach their city. Their orphan care model has been so successful that visitors from around the world visit to learn more about their process and how they can contextualize it in other contexts.

I'm thankful for leaders like Pastor Julius, who recognize the importance of fostering healthy church communities in their city. If you're ever in Kampala, make an effort to visit Watoto Church to experience this dynamic congregation that will welcome guests with open arms. Their praise and worship is world-class too!

Listen to my extended conversation with Pastor Julius by following the QR code to the video!

Fresh Emergence of Gospel City Movements

As early as 1998, Eric Swanson helped start a GCM in Boulder, Colorado, with the belief that "because cities are far larger than churches, we are writing about the kingdom and how the whole church can bring the whole Gospel—in word and deed—to the whole city."[53] Under the leadership of Kevin Palau and the Luis Palau Association, an initiative in Portland, Oregon, was formed, called CityServe, a movement that "encourages, equips, and empowers the Body of Christ to love and serve the city through united, long-term efforts focused on the greatest needs."[54] The Palau Association also helped launch City Gospel Movements, which serves hundreds of new GCMs[55] throughout the U.S. Movement.org, founded by Mac Pier and initiated by the late Tim Keller and others in New York City, also begin to initiate and serve hundreds of GCMs across America and around the world. Most recently these two major platforms have joined forces to establish the GCM

Collective, a central organizing and facilitating initiative to help support this spontaneous, growing response.

Grassroots local pastors and missional leaders have initiated new GCMs that have grown significantly. In Denver, Colorado, CityUnite "exists to help faith, government, and business leaders unite around common causes in their communities."[56] In Phoenix, Arizona, the Surge Network is working to equip, send, and bless churches to serve their communities.[57] In Texas, Christ Together Greater Austin "seeks to convene, catalyze, connect, and celebrate city wide efforts that pursue Gospel saturation."[58] In South Florida, Church United is "a partnership of local churches... joining together to transform our region."[59]

Core Identity of Gospel City Movements

These specific GCMs and many others like them share an objective level of commonality. The Gospel Movement website describes a Gospel movement as "a united, holistic, sustainable effort by the citywide Church to seek the peace and prosperity of their city."[60] Current GCMs are characterized by at least five key components: local orientation, church unity, holistic Gospel, partnering with the laity, and operational characteristics, undergirded in every case by an initial prayer movement.

1. Local orientation

Local orientation refers to a near-context focus upon the particularities of the city. GCMs share a common underlying approach and process that seeks to appropriately engage the unique context of their city with the Gospel. This fundamental process is being leveraged in order to discern identifiable strategies within specific city contexts. A GCM leader explained this approach simply as "studying their city and executing on a vision that is unique to their community."[61] To align church leaders in a city, "we challenge the leaders to ask three questions: 'What is the lostness of the city?' which relates to the spiritual component, 'What is the pain of the city?' which relates to the social component, and 'What is the brokenness of the city?' which relates to the cultural component."[62] Utilizing this common process can lead to contextual insights about what the locally felt needs of a city are:

> Maybe in Hollywood that looks like homelessness. Maybe in East Fort Lauderdale that looks like a lot of foster care people, a lot of foster kids being removed out of their homes. Maybe in some of the other regions it looks like sex trafficking. The goal is to discern what people are saying is the number one kind of felt need.[63]

City Spotlight: Martin Luther King Church Paris, France

When I think of a leader who is innovating how church can be done in the twenty-first century within a very distinct context, I think of Pastor Ivan Carluer, who pastors the Martin Luther King Church in Créteil, France.

Today, MLK Church has more than three thousand members, and they reach more than forty thousand people every week through their online services. This church is also extremely diverse, with more than 60 percent of its members being mixed. But how did Ivan build a church like this in such a complex city like Paris?

I spent my high school years in France, so I have a deep affinity for the country and its people. However, Paris is often considered one of the hardest places to plant a church. Paris has long been the center of culture through its fashion, architecture, and food. In fact, it's one of the first megacities in the world, and it's continuing to grow and expand as it becomes a global city as well.

As we think about the theology of the city, the Bible talks about how one of the major pressures in Babylon was making a name for oneself. People come from all over the world to make a name for themselves in Paris, and they have done so for centuries. Pastor Ivan came into this very complex city with an evangelical church and began confronting many of these ideologies in France.

Unlike most stories in which a pastor feels led to plant a church in a specific area, Ivan decided to map out potential locations.

"I had a map, and the map was sufficient for me. I put up the map of Paris' area, and I just put a spot on every place there is a church. I found out there was no church, almost no churches in southeast Paris." —Pastor Ivan Carluer

When he asked other pastors why no one planted a church there, they told him that it was a communist area that did not want evangelical churches in their community.

Most people would see this as a closed door, but Ivan saw it as an opportunity. However, in order for this to be a successful church, one has to be observant of the city they are in and what that city needs from the body of Christ. Here were Ivan's first observations: the city was full of young people searching for purpose; he had to be extremely relevant to the conversations going on in this part of the city; and a large part of the population were immigrants from the Caribbean and Africa.

Ivan decided to name the church Martin Luther King Church, not only to make it clear that this was an open and welcoming space for anyone but so that the mayor wouldn't block this church from being built since anything that sounded "churchy" would be denied. In missiology terms, Ivan built a contextual bridge by adapting his ecclesiology to the city's context rather than adapting the city's context to his ecclesiology.

Since Créteil is a very communist area, Ivan knew that taking care of the poor, which is what many churches focus on, would not bode well with the mayor since he could potentially feel his job being threatened. So, he focused on what the city needed: a less extremist view of religion.

Through biblical history, we see that cities do not like absolute truth. Instead, they're built on pluralism because they want everyone to feel comfortable and welcome. Even if the city was historically a Buddhist, Hindu, Muslim, or Christian place, it needs to become a place of pluralism if it wants to grow. So, there needs to be a balance in which, as an orthodox evangelical believer, you believe that Jesus is the one and only way, yet you have to approach the city from a pluralistic standpoint with a message of love like Martin Luther King had that makes peace in the city and a leader within the community.

Ivan had to find that balance as he befriended the Catholic, Jewish, and Muslim leaders within the city in order to show that they could all respect and talk with one another.

"You have to be completely sure that the Holy Spirit inside of you is stronger than any other spirit in the world....The Lord is the one taking care of the love between the other religious leaders in the community." —Pastor Ivan Carluer

With much of the population being either Jewish or Muslim, Ivan knew that 50 percent of the city would already never step foot inside the church if they saw a cross outside. He decided not to make the building look spiritual on the outside but, instead, to fill the building with great spiritual people.

From the beginning, Ivan approached the city with a humble attitude in seeking how he could serve the city. The citizens of the city are coming to church, not for religious reasons necessarily, but because they're trying to survive in the midst of an urban context. There's this theology of service that says if we're not providing value, then we almost don't deserve to exist in the city.

The name of the building is Martin Luther King Community Center, and it's open every day of the week to anyone and everyone in the community. Because of this, the mayor and other leaders within the community put millions of dollars toward building it even though the building becomes MLK Church every Sunday.

This is one of the most beautiful community centers I've seen, and it had to be since it's in Paris—the city of beauty. You have to reflect on what's important to the culture, so Ivan built a building that's beautiful enough for the city that he lives in. It has a restaurant, a gymnasium, day cares, and pantries for those in need to get food or supplies. This community center is adding so much value.

Since this building was not built out of an economic model for the church, it has allowed Ivan to have some of the best audiovisual that I've seen. Award ceremonies, artist showcases, speeches, and weddings all happen within the building. Not only is this an incredible church, but Ivan has also built a place for social good and economic good.

The city is always going to be on the edge of culture, philosophy, and progress. Paris has always been a particularly progressive city, and instead of leaning trying to react against the conversations the city is having, Ivan has decided to lean into the conversation by inviting it into the church. He does this by inviting non-Christian professionals to talk about specific topics that he will then preach over. Many pastors are scared to do this, but cities like Paris are constantly asking questions, and by not ignoring those questions, you open a door for them to step into a new way of thinking. As we are obedient in having these hard conversations, the Holy Spirit is obedient to show up and guide those topics, no matter how difficult it might seem.

Ivan has found a way to change the nature of the church because he hasn't just given his congregation a place to gather, but he has empowered them to understand that they are planted in a city and that, as the body of Christ, it is their job to be salt and light within their community. In fact, Ivan encourages his congregation to only come a couple of times a month to the physical church itself and to host meetings in their homes with neighbors or family on the other Sundays. He's seen exponential growth.

"We started a new small 'church' like that every week. So it will be more than a hundred in only one year.... Every week we open a new one. Why? Because of congruency. Because of relevancy. You think about the church in a new way—the same spirit, same Jesus, but a new model." —Pastor Ivan Carluer

This is an unusual ecclesiology, but he's encouraging his congregants to realize that the building is not the church. He's discipling them to know that they are Kingdom citizens and that they're to go into the world, into their homes, and into their city with God's love.

What Ivan is doing is not evolutionary; it's revolutionary. Pastoring an effective church in the city can really be seen through Ivan's life, through his journey, through what God is doing, and through MLK Church. Young people are attracted to the city, but so many of them will lose their faith if we don't present that relevant, dynamic interpretation of the Scripture for the times they're living in, so I'm thankful for Ivan doing just that in France.

Listen to my extended conversation with Pastor Ivan by following the QR code to the video!

2. Church unity

GCMs share a purposeful unity for city transformation. This unity is upheld by both a theological conviction (John 17:20–23; Eph. 4:4–6) and a character focus of humility and servanthood. GCM leaders thus summarize their efforts by advocating that "we are together for the Gospel."[64] Another GCM leader reported that "we boiled our vision down to six words: 'The church united for the city.'"[65] Based on this spiritual conviction of church unity, the arrangement of GCMs tend to be widely inclusive of diverse church denominations and expressions:

> The vision is not for just more churches or more leaders of one type or one denomination, but rather a vision for the whole city. We would argue that to reach a city is going to require a coalition of churches across multiple denominations and expressions.[66]

Relational trust is the stitching that holds the living fabric of GCMs together. This includes the process of building private relational trust, which has everything to do with establishing and nurturing trusted relationships between Christian leaders. Relational trust also includes the idea of developing public relational trust, which is concerned about the relationship and credibility between Christian leaders in the movement and civic leaders in the city.

Another critical feature of church unity is that GCMs help local churches and nonprofits collaborate for

The church is at its best when it's both demonstrating and proclaiming the Gospel.

missional impact. A GCM leader explained, "We believe that when we can create a platform that drives people toward deepening relational unity and trust, that the fruit of that will be transformation in our city....As pastors and church leaders come together to pray, build relationships, and trust, over time they will mobilize themselves to collaborate."[67] Church unity leads to missional collaboration. The importance of unity is seen, therefore, not as an end unto itself, but rather as something that is both galvanized by and purposed for missional impact. This is further explained by another GCM leader:

> Faith communities will come together around mission. They won't come together as just unity for the sake of unity; it isn't sustainable. But unity around purpose works. And so you have to have...a common bull's-eye to go after.[68]

3. Holistic Gospel

GCMs engage their cities with a holistic Gospel that includes both word (i.e., evangelism) and deed (i.e., service). As one GCM leader explained, "I think the church is at its best when it's both demonstrating and proclaiming the Gospel....That is when the church is at its healthiest; it's when the Gospel is at its healthiest."[69] A growing concern among city leaders is the natural pull away from intentional evangelism and proclamation. The cities are open to societal transformation, but only the Church can place a clear declaration of the Gospel story at the center or our world. This is how one GCM leader explained this process: "We'll be more effective in our evangelism and our unity if we can build it around serving the city."[70] Engaging the city with a holistic Gospel also means working with civic leaders to serve the city in practical ways, such as helping in the areas of homelessness, hunger, health care, school partnerships, foster care, refugee care, and job creation.

4. Partnering with the laity

GCM leaders are expressing the urgent need for including marketplace members and their work into a more holistic and integral vision for what it means to embody a faithful Gospel witness that serves the common good of the city. This includes recovering and championing a vision for the idea of vocation, which celebrates virtually all forms of work as existing for God's glory and the public's good. This is how one GCM leader articulated the importance of integrating faith and work into the larger paradigm of GCMs:

> The challenge is for pastors to help their people to see themselves through the larger vision of what God is accomplishing in the city, so that they can then join in this process. So how do pastors connect with their people to disciple them in their vocations to the larger vision that we feel God is trusting us with and calling us to here in the city?[71]

Recognizing and incorporating marketplace members into the broader framework of GCMs involves "connecting key business leaders and Kingdom capital to entrepreneurial common good solutions to solve the city's problems."[72] Empowering and engaging believers in marketplace sectors is beginning to revolutionize GCMs. Part of this transformation is being realized as lay believers are rediscovering themselves and their vocations as essential, rather than tangential, to what God is doing in their cities. As GCMs are championing the integral role that marketplace members have in the cause of the Gospel for the city, business leaders are being stimulated to "think about their faith, not just as a way to survive, but the way they can utilize their faith to create a more thriving city."[73]

5. Operational characteristics

There are several core operational characteristics that GCMs have in common.

- GCMs seek to add value and mobilize local churches and nonprofits in the city. This fundamentally means that GCMs are situated in a serving and convening role toward local churches and nonprofits in their cities. GCM leaders thus explain their agenda: "We equip and resource the Church to accomplish a larger city vision."[74] By adding value to the local churches and nonprofits in the city, GCMs "help them do ministry more richly" and "amplify the work and serve the already-work that is being done."[75] GCMs are adding value across a spectrum of categories, such as church planting, financial literacy, and family counseling. GCMs also seek to mobilize local churches and nonprofits in the city toward greater ministry effectiveness. That is, rather than trying to do ministry directly, GCMs help to convene and mobilize other churches, marketplaces, and ministries in the city.
- As GCMs embrace a convening role to connect, collaborate, and celebrate ministry in the city, there is a careful dance that takes place between the broader GCM and its constituent parts, composed of local churches and nonprofits. With the overarching desire to "create and see a city flourish and look at how we create a Gospel ecosystem here in this region with all of its components,"[76] GCM leaders carefully operate without trying to overtly direct or control ministry. The consensus of thought is that "the best initiatives are the ones that come up, they bubble up from the ground level."[77] GCM leaders are thus purposeful about what kind of operating

principles might foster authentic collaboration and buy-in from individuals toward a larger city movement.

This principle recognizes that not all organizations can or should do the same thing, but rather when each church or ministry focuses on the specific areas of engagement within their respective range of expertise and potential contribution, the combined outcome will be more effective. "Pursuing a shared outcome does not require churches to pursue shared activities." This gives latitude and flexibility across the wide spectrum of theological, cultural, and sizes of churches and ministries that GCMs serve. At the same time, it ensures that the diversity of activities is anchored within a common agenda that stakeholders themselves have highlighted as essential to the transformation of the city.

- GCMs engage in continuous rhythms of purposeful communication. At least two basic leadership structures are central to GCMs' operational characteristics. At the core of the leadership there is normally a smaller group of executive leaders, variously termed "senior catalysts," "steering team," "executive leaders," "governing board," and "city fathers/mothers." On a broader level there is a larger associate group typically made up of senior pastors and marketplace, nonprofit, and influential leaders. The way in which communication happens within GCMs is best understood in light of these main leadership groups.

Achieving Missional Sustainability

A crucial underlining thread must run throughout the five core identities of GCMs in order to achieve missional sustainability, and that's a reverse flow of energy. Have you ever been in a store or hotel where there is a waterfall feature? The cascading water looks and sounds pleasant and creates a sort of ambiance that adds value to the location. Behind the scenes of this water feature, there's a pump, a gauge, and a system making sure the water level remains at an acceptable level. It's an in-tune cycle. If any part were to suddenly malfunction, this could cause disastrous effects as water would flood everywhere causing damage. In the same way a waterfall feature contains many parts that work together to both let the water fall *and* feed back into the system, we, too, must ensure there is a reverse flow of energy when it comes to mission and ministry.

The reverse flow of energy model relays that for sustainable transformation to exists, there needs to be three primary agencies: missional individuals, missional communities, and missional ecosystems. These three agencies share equal responsibility to secure a sustainable influence in a geographical region. They must all work together to create enriching and healthy environments. It is not a war of differing agendas. Instead of an agency putting a demand on the other to come and serve their agenda, the goal should be to empower the engaging agency to fulfill Kingdom impact in the region as collaborators.

This is how the reversal of energy works: the missional individual serves the church, which is the missional community. The church then mobilizes and models missions to the city through their service, and the city becomes a missional ecosystem that collaborates with and celebrates the church. Meanwhile, the church continues to empower the missional individuals as they're empowered by the city. This is how a healthy flow and reversal of energy should exist within a GCM.

Misalignment can have disastrous effects. The church must position itself as a "missional community." Otherwise, an involved leader simply feels validation from

Pursuing a shared outcome does not require churches to pursue shared activities.

their actions, instead of the local church actually being mobilized to see transformation.

There are also three dimensions that church leaders grapple with throughout their church's journey. They need to make sure their church is growing, healthy, and on mission. Ensuring that all three of these aspects are happening at once is often one of the hardest tasks to manage.

City Spotlight: Substance Church Minneapolis, Minnesota

"If God has given me a heart for a city, do I plant a church in the suburbs first or go straight to the city?"

This is a question I am asked by church groups and missionaries around the world. Usually, it's because suburban areas will have more settled, church-going families with an openness to tithing, as opposed to starting right at the core of a city, which is typically more closed off to churches and extremely transient.

Pastors Peter and Carolyn Haas are two very close friends and incredible leaders who not only had to make this decision but now pastor Substance Church, a multisite church in Minneapolis, Minnesota, with five locations and more than eight thousand attendees.

Before Substance Church, Peter and Carolyn pastored a megachurch in Wisconsin for nine years. During a speaking engagement at the University of Minnesota, Peter read an article stating that Minneapolis was becoming unchurched at one of the fastest rates in the United States. At the time, less than 1 percent of people under forty went to any church of any kind. This is heartbreaking, especially in a city where there are sixteen universities and over two million people under forty.

Peter's heart was moved, so he and Carolyn began praying and fasting, seeking guidance on whether they should leave their church to plant a new church in Minneapolis.

"Literally a woman came up to us in the middle of our church, and she said, 'Pastor Peter, I had the craziest dream that you and Carolyn resigned from this church and moved to a suburb in Minneapolis. I don't know if you've ever heard of it. It's called Roseville, and you planted a church, and God blessed it.' And then she goes, 'But I know you'd never do that.' And she just kind of laughed it off. Believe it or not, that happened three times as we were praying and fasting, to the point where I knew this was God calling us to start from scratch." —Pastor Peter Haas

Peter and Carolyn planted their church in Roseville with the Association of Related Churches, an organization that supports church planters and pastors from various backgrounds to spread the message of Jesus. They received various methodological advice when it came to planting in the city.

Since Peter and Carolyn were experienced senior pastors, they took a risk by planting in a second-ring suburb of Minneapolis. By doing this, they not only went after the demographic they felt called to but also became culture shapers in the city by being within a university area. Their church appealed to young college students and soon launched into a portable multisite system.

At one point, Peter was preaching seven services in four portable locations, and some of those locations were 80 percent new to Christ, and he didn't even know if half of his church had actually crossed the threshold of conversion. Along with the increase came growing pains, one being a lack of mature believers to mentor others.

"We were so effective with unchurched people that we were almost too effective. To the point where it was total chaos. It was a house of cards, and so I needed more disciplers." —Pastor Peter Haas

With many new believers, Peter and Carolyn saw the need to welcome and attract more spiritually mature adults into the congregation to help guide and mentor the younger generation.

This phase was also a challenge financially. They were functioning under an unstable church model because they were reaching millennial college students who didn't have a strong Christian tithing culture, and many people were moving away. They were caring for two thousand attendees with the income of a two hundred–member church.

"When we grew by two hundred, we actually grew by six hundred and lost four hundred to churn. Either they fell away from the Lord or they got transferred, since Minneapolis is a Fortune 500 recruiting hub, and they would move." —Pastor Peter Haas

Peter realized that they needed to invite more financially stable families to balance out the college demographic. Soon Substance Church began receiving a lot of born-again parents of Millennial Christian kids. These parents were shocked that their kids were going to church again so they began attending as well. At some level, they had two distinct congregations that they were trying to pastor at the same time, and a generational divide began to happen. The younger generation wanted the fresh and modern, and the older generation leaned more traditional. Thankfully, the parents became so excited by the fruitfulness of the church that this overshadowed other preferences like worship styles. This season is when Substance Church became sustainable.

"We ended up launching a northern suburban campus that started paying for our urban campuses. So it was almost like a suburban, urban symbiotic relationship.... Multisite enabled us to balance out the problems of the urban model." —Pastor Peter Haas

Young adults would meet their spouses in their urban church, get married, have kids, and decide to move to the suburbs and join their suburban campus. Meanwhile, the kids of the suburban campuses would grow up, move into the city, and join the urban campus.

This verse from the Book of Jeremiah is often quoted, "I have a hope and a future." It's crucial to understand its true context—this was Jeremiah's message to the subcultural Jews living in Babylon during their exile. Instead of resisting their situation, Jeremiah urges the community to build a life in Babylon. He encourages them to invest in the city, to purchase land and homes, and to raise their families. This narrative highlights the importance of laying down roots as a community, a critical element for fostering the substance and sustainability of a church in an urban setting.

"No matter where our location is, what we do is we target universal youth culture. We always allow our eighteen- to twenty-one-year-olds to define our Sunday morning culture, wherever it is....We're doing church for your unchurched neighbor. And you'll never understand why we do what we do unless you regularly invite your unchurched neighbor." —Pastor Peter Haas

Peter recommends most church planters start in the suburbs and then grow to the city. "If you start in the suburbs, still be thinking about urban, universal youth culture of the city, so that when you do make that jump, you're capable of doing it without having all these core value alarms," he said.

Reaching the city also involves being prepared to face widespread tragedies that you usually wouldn't encounter as much in rural areas. Substance Church experienced this firsthand when George Floyd was murdered just six blocks away from their Downtown campus.

The city always faced profound racial disparities, compounded by tension with the police force. The video recording of Floyd's murder, which went viral, triggered widespread protests and riots that spread globally. The pandemic exacerbated the situation as COVID lockdowns disproportionately affected the urban core, leaving many without jobs and causing significant social disruption.

Before COVID, their Northtown campus had a food distribution program that served up to four thousand individuals per week. Though this campus was the hub of their food distribution, they would also constantly take trucks full of groceries into the city and distribute it at their Downtown location. When COVID lockdowns began, the government was trying to stop them from distributing food to those in need, saying they were causing harm. The mayor even threatened to send police to arrest their volunteers.

Then, when the George Floyd riots came all the way to Substance Church, Peter was afraid it would be burned down, but the local community protected the church. Why? Because they had seen the church distribute groceries for years. Their building ended up becoming an outreach hub to the whole city, and then the very government that was threatening to arrest them was calling asking for help to stop the chaos. This is what it means to be the body of Christ within the city, to be a beacon of hope in the midst of darkness and unrest.

We often say churches are transformational agents within the city, but what really makes a church transformational within an urban community are the healthy families within it. When I think of Substance Church, I think of a community of faith that stands up for the truth while knowing how to make truth relevant and dynamic for a postmodern demographic. They are an incredible community of accountability, and they've found ways to navigate tension points.

Substance Church has found a way to live out a theology of faith, hope, and love in the midst of its unique urban context, and it did so by being a small-group cell church model with a weekend experience.

"In order to survive, we've had to figure out that equilibrium of how do we have a place where seekers can explore faith anonymously on a Sunday and yet fall down the funnel into the more gritty, confessional, ground yourself in Scripture, wrestle with God moments, which happen within small groups." —Pastor Peter Haas

What sets Substance Church apart is its approach to handling hot-button topics, which are often addressed within small groups, thereby avoiding political divides within the congregation. They have been remarkably effective in connecting with the LGBT community while staying true to the holiness tradition. Their message emphasizes that all of us are sexually broken, struggling with desires that don't align with biblical parameters and lacking a "Godward" orientation. The central theme is the need for Christ to bring about inner transformation. This approach is non-offensive and piques people's interest while leaving everyone with a sense of dignity, respect, honor, and hope.

Peter's story is truly exceptional. It's remarkable to witness how he and Carolyn began their journey as a young couple, answering God's call to Minneapolis and then developing a model that can be replicated in progressive first-world cities. We often say churches are transformational agents within the city, but what really makes a church transformational within an urban community are the healthy families within it.

I encourage everyone to visit Minneapolis and witness firsthand the incredible work that God is accomplishing through Peter and Carolyn. I know that Minneapolis, once known as a church graveyard, is emerging as a vibrant example of a place with faith-filled communities.

Listen to my extended conversation with Pastor Peter by following the QR code to the video!

The Science of Collective Impact

Sociology can help us fine-tune our missiological perspectives and methods of engagement. The science of Collective Impact (CI) offers a useful organizing framework. The striking similarities between CI and GCMs predict they have good potential for theoretical and operational synergy.

CI was first introduced in 2011 by John Kania, managing director at Foundation Strategy Group, and Mark Kramer, Harvard University's John F. Kennedy School of Government.[78] The growth of CI grew out of a need to more effectively address diverse social problems that are inherently large and complex. CI stands in contrast to historically conventional approaches that can be referred to as isolated impact. The basic strategy of isolated impact is to fund and leverage single organizations that by themselves attempt to influence social problems. In contrast, CI is defined as the long-term "commitment of a group of important actors from different sectors to a common agenda for solving a specific social problem," using a structured form of collaboration.[79] CI has contributed to sustained improvements and is rapidly gaining use around the world to address large-scale adaptive social problems.[80] CI is a versatile systematic framework that strategically engages diverse community sectors to impact long-term outcomes.[81] As an organizational and operational framework, this model exemplifies fruitful potential for GCMs to adapt and use.

CI is distinct from different kinds of traditional collaboration, representing a more disciplined, systematic, and higher-performing approach to achieving large-scale social impact. As an organizational system, CI incorporates five core conditions that together encourage deeper organizational alignment that can lead to more powerful outcomes:

1. Common agenda: Sharing a vision for change that includes a common understanding of the problem and agreed-upon approach and activities for solving the problem.
2. Shared measurement systems: Having agreed-upon ways that outcomes will be measured and reported.
3. Mutually reinforcing activities: Coordinating a set of differentiated activities through a conjoined plan of action.
4. Continuous communication: Maintaining consistent and open communication over time among key participants within and across contributing organizations.
5. Backbone support organizations: Ongoing support by an independent staff who is dedicated to serving and managing the initiative.[82]

As GCMs are considered in light of the organizational framework provided by CI, it seems that on many occasions GCMs are paralleling analogous kinds of organization work without necessarily having the developed framework and descriptive language of CI. From an organizational and operational perspective, the CI model possesses a disciplined level of systematic collaboration that could be appropriately applied to GCMs to help launch, sustain, and grow them. The five core conditions of CI thus comprise a strategic organizational framework that could be modified and utilized to enhance the growth and productivity of GCMs. As you can see, CI is a robust framework that usually requires significant effort to pull off, which is why I recommend anyone interested to also do further research into the latest and more minimalistic refinement of CI referred to as minimal viable consortia.

For Such a Time as This

The recent uprising of GCMs is both a natural and supernatural response to our current context. Cities are rapidly growing and will continue to be the dominant space where humanity resides. Cities hold particular social, cultural, and spiritual powers that require specific and localized responses from the Church. Throughout history, in response to His Spirit's guidance, God's people have made missiological shifts in light of the sociological realities the Church has faced. From Pentecost to the present, we have witnessed that "the historical Church cannot do without the constant renewal of its form. Renewal of form implies change of form by means of human decision and responsibility....Changing times demands changing forms."[83] The changing times of our day and subsequent emergence of GCMs appear to be most needed and proportional in ratio to the size and progressive nature of the cities that are being impacted by globalization's sociocultural diversity and the pluralism that accompany it.

Today GCMs are attempting to understand what is happening in our cities by discerning in community what the Spirit is directing the Church in the city to do in response. The process appears to be producing clear spiritual, social, and cultural outcomes for the Church to pursue. This process is not unlike the intentionality of prior awakenings and revivals that identified particular activities and outcomes to pursue in response to their realities.

"The more sober have learned from history that there are, what Emile Durkheim called, 'moments of effervescence,' 'periods of create and renewal,' times when people 'are brought into more intimate relations with one another, when meetings and assemblies are more frequent, relationships more solid and the exchange of ideas more active,'" Martin E. Morty wrote in the foreword to William G. McLoughlin's book *Revivals, Awakenings, and Reform.*[84]

Awakenings have been the shaping power of American culture from its inception. McLoughlin explains: "They are not brief outbursts of mass emotionalism by one group or another but profound cultural transformations affecting all Americans and extending over a generation or more. Awakenings begin in periods of cultural distortion and grave personal stress, when we lose faith in the legitimacy of our norms, the viability of our institutions, and the authority of our leaders in church and state. They eventuate in basic restructurings of our institutions and redefinitions of our social goals. Great awakenings are not periods of social neurosis (though they begin in times of cultural confusion). They are times of revitalization. They are therapeutic and cathartic, not pathological. They restore our cultural verve and our self-confidence, helping us to maintain faith in ourselves, our ideals, and our 'covenant with

God' even while they compel us to reinterpret that covenant in the light of new experience."[85]

True revitalizations not only respond to and affect cultural shifts, but they also reshape the Church's own practical ecclesiology and form. This appears to be happening in a more localized and measured way, in a growing post-denominational context with the emergence of a new theology of the city and direct Spirit-led initiatives like GCMs.

Your Contributions to the Peace and Prosperity of the City

We all have the responsibility to be fruitfully and faithfully present in our cities. Largely, this begins by opening our eyes to the realities around us and acting upon the Holy Spirit's prompting.

Several years ago, I was driving to work on the same familiar road I always traveled. Stopped at a light near my office, I heard the Holy Spirit say, "Take a right turn." What I witnessed changed my life and the ministry of OneHope. My unexpected right turn landed me in an urban community called Avondale. As I drove the streets that day, I saw drug abuse, prostitutes soliciting customers in the middle of the day, and school-age children roaming the streets as a handful of adults watched passively.

I was overcome with emotion, and I pulled to the side of the road to process what I was feeling. I felt angry and deeply convicted. Right across the street from my work were people suffering, trapped by their circumstances, and I hadn't seen the hopelessness in my community. I was angry at the waste of human potential. I thought of the children and how they were trapped in a society prison of poverty, abuse, and neglect.

Seeing the brokenness in my community, I determined to do something. When I arrived at the office, I began to explain to my team members what I had witnessed. At OneHope, we began to research Avondale and build a plan for how we could bring others along to begin making a positive impact in the community. I felt sure that as the president of a global ministry delivering a biblical message of purpose and hope to children all over the world, God had intended for me to take that right turn in order to discover this patch of needy children located in my office's back yard.

We learned Avondale was labeled "Struggling Urban Diversity" by the Percept Group, but there was also a very low population of married people and two-parent families. Avondale also ranked in the bottom 1 percent of U.S. neighborhoods for safety with 776 crimes per square mile per year, in contrast with the U.S. average of 50 per square mile. We even went door to door to personally ask the residents what kind of help families in their community needed.

We created goals and designed a program that would achieve the desired outcomes for this specific community, and then we sought out partner ministries and churches to come alongside our efforts to sustain the relationships and work we were starting in Avondale. The community now has access to a new charter school, English as a second language classes, health fairs, interview preparation, and mentoring. We're seeing the fruit of these efforts. Avondale residents have hope for a better future, and individuals like Haylee are finding hope and healing in desperate situations.

Haylee's grandmother worked multiple jobs to provide for the family, and enrolled Haylee in the charter school hosted in the same building as OneHope. As a safe and secure place for her, Haylee began to grow and flourish. She was making great strides in her education and personal growth when her world shattered as she received news that her mother had died from a drug

May we be faithfully present in our cities and attuned to how the Lord would have us act.

overdose. Friends of the school rallied around Haylee and her grandmother. Haylee participated in free grief counseling, and complete strangers raised money to give to Haylee's grandma for her care to alleviate some of the stressors. A short time later, a fire broke out in their home. Again, the community responded to meet the need. Haylee and her grandmother have people in their lives who care for their well-being. I heard that Haylee has initiated a volunteer group of her fellow students to clean up the beaches of her city.

When I think back to that day I first drove through Avondale, I wonder if I saw Haylee. What if I hadn't taken that right turn? What if I had never witnessed the great need in my city and decided to take action?

I encourage you to create space in your life to be nudged by the Holy Spirit in a direction that you may have never considered. May we be faithfully present in our cities and attuned to how the Lord would have us act.

City Spotlight: Cathedral of Faith (Catedral de la Fe) Buenos Aires, Argentina

One of my closest friends is Osvaldo Carnival, who is leading an incredibly impactful church in his city and nation.

I've known Osvaldo for over thirty years, and this incredible man of God—along with his wife, Alejandra, who is an amazing woman of God—had the vision to start a church in Buenos Aires, Argentina, which began with a mere ten members. Their passion for evangelism, coupled with incredible leadership, has now grown this church from ten to tens of thousands, with multiple campuses, thanks to their faith and willingness to innovate and extend their ministries.

Situated on the western shore of the Río de la Plata, Buenos Aires is one of the most populous cities in South America. The city's architecture is a blend of various influences, reflecting its history of change, immigration, and cultural uniqueness. Buenos Aires often draws comparisons to European cities, earning it the nickname the "Paris of South America." Buenos Aires is not only the political and economic center of the country but also serves as a cultural hub that showcases the nation's rich history, traditions, and dynamic contemporary life.

The city of Buenos Aires includes a metropolitan area of nearly twenty million people. Their work began in the middle of the city, where almost three million Argentinians call home. Osvaldo started Cathedral of Faith on the streets of the city, preaching outdoors for six months. God worked from the first night, with five people praying to receive Jesus.

One mother and her son were a block away from the church's meeting. They were next to the train tracks, waiting to jump on the tracks as it passed to commit suicide. As they walked toward the tracks, they heard a worship song. The child ran off toward the event, and they ended up sitting in the first row of the meeting. After the service, they went forward and shared their story, crying tears of joy. They believed in Jesus, and He saved their lives physically and spiritually. This moment became a sign for the young church.

Twenty years later, three blocks from where that situation occurred, the church had over twenty thousand people meeting for worship. They saw miracles every night that brought people to Jesus. Pastor Osvaldo has now served at that church for nearly forty years alongside Alejandra and their three children.

Today, Cathedral of Faith reaches thousands of people each week through five weekend worship services at its main locations as one of the largest churches in Argentina. Additional campuses reach thousands more worshippers at more than twenty locations across Argentina, in addition to Bolivia and Barcelona, Spain. Pastor Osvaldo also serves as a member of the board of directors of ACIERA, a network of more than fifteen thousand churches in Argentina. Pastor Osvaldo shared about the waves of the Holy Spirit he and other pastors have experienced in Argentina over the past four decades, including a wave of healing.

"The same miracles were happening in other places. Then we would have a season of deep worship, and then a season of anointing and renewal. The last season was about multiplication and renewal." —Pastor Osvaldo Carnival

What's interesting about Osvaldo's story is that awakenings like these usually don't happen in megacities, but he, along with several other pastors in Argentina, were able to catch waves of the Holy Spirit together, as the leaders sought unity.

Osvaldo believes one reason the church has thrived is that through the leading of the Holy Spirit he has been able to build relationships with the other churches in the city, no matter their denomination. Unity fosters real trust.

"There is another wave from the Holy Spirit that is unity, that has allowed us to walk together, leaving behind egos and vanity. I've had the opportunity to travel around the world, and I didn't see unity of this kind outside of Argentina. Unity has no denomination." —Pastor Osvaldo Carnival

The relationships Osvaldo has built with the other city pastors have nurtured a special kind of unity and trust—not just unity for the sake of unity, but unity for the sake of mission. By working together, they've been able to align their hearts on how they're reaching their city and nation with Jesus; these are friendships with a purpose.

In 2020, the COVID pandemic struck, offering a unique challenge for the church. This was an incredible opportunity for Osvaldo and his church to serve the city at a moment when everyone was scared and isolated. The congregation opened its building as a vaccination center. In three months, over three hundred thousand people passed through the building. Church members offered food, coffee, prayer, and had numerous opportunities to minister to people who had never attended their church. The outreach had a major impact on the city during a difficult time. Despite controversies over the pandemic, Cathedral of Faith used every resource possible to share God's hope.

Though this is a very different version of evangelism than when Osvaldo preached on a street corner over forty years ago, it's an incredible example of how Cathedral of Faith is using every resource available within the city to preach.

"There are always new ways and opportunities to evangelize in the city; you just have to be sensitive to the Holy Spirit in order to find them and use them wisely."
—Pastor Osvaldo Carnival

This is a vision of the theology of service. It really helps guide how we use influence in the city. This brings me back to Jesus saying to be the salt and light in your city, the leaven within the bread. There is tension between being a faithful presence in the city and changing the city. When we understand transformation, it doesn't mean taking over the city; it means serving the city.

I've personally seen Osvaldo go on this journey for over thirty years, and now I'm seeing how Sebastian, his son, is building bridges between generations and helping to connect Osvaldo's and my generation to younger generations. Osvaldo and Sebastian have a deep intentionality when it comes to intergenerational ministry; they are empowering the next generation's voice in the city so they can navigate our changing world within God's truth.

It's vital to learn from the experiences of the other generations and discover the challenges they've faced. Together, we can be stronger and gain wisdom. We can also avoid the mistakes of the past by learning from those who have gone before us. The best ministry happens with friendships, not just friendships within your own peer group but friendships across generations.

"I believe it's important to have a multigenerational vision. There are some that will put all of the emphasis on the new generation, but we cannot leave behind the other generation. I see it as multigenerational—that we can walk all together." —Pastor Osvaldo Carnival

Staying relevant is essential to having an impact on the city, and as an older pastor, Osvaldo has found numerous ways to connect with and serve the next generation.

He has harnessed multimedia platforms, including a TV show produced by CBN International for broadcasting and a radio show to amplify the reach and impact of the ministry's impact. He also has a YouTube channel with over 120,000 subscribers, where he reacts as a pastor to different pop culture topics. Osvaldo's videos are gaining a lot of traction with the next generation and are giving them a more biblical perspective on today's culture.

Osvaldo's church has a ministry called Cathedral Kids as well, which helps engage children and families with the Bible. Its goal is for young people to know God in an experiential way, understanding that they are a reflection of God's love for humankind. Cathedral of Faith also has an educational program (Seminario Bíblico) where students interact with different leaders, pastors, and professors who teach courses with biblical, theological, and practical subjects to help Christians grow spiritually, excel intellectually, and be equipped to serve God with excellence.

Next, Cathedral of Faith seeks to extend the legacy of its impact to future generations in the city. The government has asked the church to establish the first evangelical university in the city. OneHope, Pastor Osvaldo, and a Christian university in the United States engaged in cabinet-level discussions with the government of Argentina to lay the groundwork for the establishment of the nation's first Protestant evangelical university. This remarkable initiative marks a significant milestone in the collaboration between these organizations and the Argentine government.

The pursuit of establishing a new university requires a chartering process. God has miraculously made a way for a university charter to be approved! The envisioned plan involves utilizing the Buenos Aires campus as the focal point of the university, leveraging its robust infrastructure and capabilities. The aspiration extends beyond geographical confines, as educational opportunities are set to expand across Latin America through strategically positioned church-based extension sites and innovative online education platforms. This comprehensive approach underscores the commitment to providing accessible and impactful education throughout the region.

Cathedral of Faith seeks to deepen its work in Buenos Aires and throughout Latin America. This monumental undertaking not only represents a testament to longstanding relationships and dedicated service but also reveals the power of education to transform lives and empower communities. The steps toward establishing the first Protestant evangelical university in Argentina stand as a testament to the unwavering dedication to sharing God's hope with the world.

Even though Osvaldo has come a long way from preaching on a street corner, the mission continues with the same passion for service, whether on the street or launching a university. I am so thankful for Pastor Osvaldo, his family, and his team, as their goal of impacting the city and nation extends far beyond one person or position; they're focused on training pastors and church leaders to transform the city of Buenos Aires and reach the world with the good news of Jesus.

Listen to my extended conversation with Pastor Osvaldo and his son by following the QR code to the video!

Go Into All the World

I hope you've enjoyed this journey from the biblical origins of the city all the way to our current context. I pray that as you've read and reflected, you now have a more robust theology of the city and understand the role of the Church and your personal *missio Dei* in advancing His Kingdom.

For my daughter Natasha's graduation, I bundled together all my notes, texts, letters, and journal entries from three years of journeying with her and bound them together and called it *Oh Daughter of Zion*. In prayer, I entrust to you the same commission I bestowed on her upon her entrance into the city several years ago:

> Now that you have purified yourselves by obeying the truth so that you have sincere love for each other, love one another deeply.

—1 Peter 1:22

The loneliness of the city is perpetuated by a paradox of anonymity—so many people living in proximity that have little time or feeling for each other. People come to the city to belong and find themselves very alone.

The Church is invented to be a community of love that provides belonging. It should be the oasis of salt and light that preserves and enlightens the city from all its degradation, humiliation, and darkness. It requires a daily commitment of love to fellow believers that disarms Nimrod's legacy of domination and replaces it with a security of love and belonging.

> Above all, love each other deeply, because love covers over a multitude of sins. Offer hospitality to one another without grumbling. Each of you should use whatever gift you have received to serve others, as faithful stewards of God's grace.
>
> —1 Peter 4:8–10

My daughter, seek Christ's bride in the city; find a loving community and serve it. Without the family of God, you become part of the city that will accept what it needs from you, consuming your gifts, talents, and beauty, giving only its material, fleeting goods in exchange, until you become merchandise yourself. The city cannot love you; only He can.

You can find joy in the city because you have faith, hope, love, meaning, purpose, and belonging. The city is powerful, but these things, nurtured in you by the power of His Spirit, are more so. You don't need to reject the city; you

> must perpetually interpret it against the living and active Word of God.
>
> "Go into all the world" means going into the city, and it means being intentional about going into every sphere of life and every social structure—not to dominate it but to be light in the midst of every dark corner of the city. Excellence in the city brings you wealth, power, and status; the non-corruptive use of these elements is the greatest witness and the greatest challenge we can ever face. Wealth must become charity, power must surrender, and status must become inclusion, not exclusion. This is about you, my daughter, building a new city, a spiritual city residing in the midst of the earthly city, a counterculture promoting community over anonymity, contentment over advancement, and selflessness over selfishness.

You must be faithfully present in the city, but not of the city. You are part of an inaugurated eschatology that has begun but is not yet fulfilled. You are a foretaste of the New City, but you are not it; it comes with Christ. Babylon will be no more; the New Jerusalem will come down from heaven. The paradise of the garden man lost, but God will take what he has done—the city—and make it perfect. All things work together for good. What Satan intended for evil, God will establish for good. The garden is gone. Long live the city of our God, the New Jerusalem, that will come down from heaven.

ABOUT THE AUTHOR

Rob Hoskins is the president of OneHope, a global ministry that has reached more than two billion children and youth with God's Word worldwide since 1987. Born to missionary parents, Hoskins spent his formative years in the Middle East and France, which instilled in him a deep passion for cross-cultural ministry. Hoskins holds a doctor of ministry in world missions and cross-cultural studies from Gordon-Conwell Theological Seminary.

Since taking leadership of OneHope in 2004, he has continued to advance the vision of "God's Word. Every Child." by partnering with local churches to help reach over two billion children and youth worldwide with a contextualized presentation of God's Word. In addition to extensive print and film programs, Hoskins has overseen the expansion into digital with the *Bible App for Kids* and *Kids Bible Experience*, developed in partnership with YouVersion, as well as numerous other evangelism, discipleship, and leadership-development initiatives.

Beyond his role at OneHope, Hoskins serves as a senior adviser to the World Evangelical Alliance, is a member of the Empowered21 Global Council, and is dedicated to training emerging Christian leaders through Southeastern University's Doctor of Missiology program.

Hoskins is the author of several books, including *Change Your World*, coauthored with John C. Maxwell. Hoskins is committed to equipping leaders to make a Kingdom impact through strategic vision and practical action. Hoskins and his wife, Kim, have two daughters and four grandchildren. Together they are passionate about their mission to "build young leaders and serve great leaders."

ENDNOTES

1. Missiology is the study of Christian missions.
2. Robert D. Hoskins, "The Identity and Organization of Gospel City Movements in the United States" (DMin. diss. Gordon-Conwell Theological Seminary, May 2019), https://archive.org/details/2019HoskinsRobert
3. "Lesson Plans on Human Population and Demographic Studies," Population Reference Bureau, accessed December 14,2021, https://www.prb.org/humanpopulation/.
4. "World Population by Year," Worldometer, accessed March 3, 2021, https://web.archive.org/web/20210301224622/https://www.worldometers.info/world-population/world-population-by-year/.
5. "Lesson Plans on Human Population and Demographic Studies," Population Reference Bureau.
6. The population shifts from rural areas to urban areas (i.e., cities).
7. Jon M. Dennis, *Christ + City: Why the Greatest Need of the City Is the Greatest News of All* (Wheaton, IL: Crossway, 2013), 11.
8. The interaction, integration, and complex connectivity among people from different places in the world.
9. Ray Bakke, A *Theology as Big as the City* (Downers Grove, IL: InterVarsity Press, 1997), 13.

10. The coexistence of different types of people who have different religious beliefs and cultural values, living within the confines of a common society.
11. Tim Keller, "To Transform a City," *Christianity Today*, accessed March 7, 2021, https://web.archive.org/web/20210420142956/https://www.christianitytoday.com/pastors/2011/winter/tim-keller-transform-city.html.
12. Timothy Keller, *Center Church: Doing Balanced, Gospel-Centered Ministry in Your City* (Grand Rapids, MI: Zondervan, 2012), 368.
13. Bakke, *A Theology as Big as the City*, 14.
14. Robert C. Linthicum, *City of God, City of Satan: A Biblical Theology of the Urban City* (Grand Rapids, MI: Zondervan, 1991), 20.
15. Jacques Ellul, *The Meaning of the City* (Eugene, OR: Wipf and Stock Publishers, 2011), 15.
16. Timothy Keller, *Loving the City: Doing Balanced, Gospel-Centered Ministry in Your City* (Grand Rapids, MI: Zondervan, 2016), 120.
17. James Davison Hunter, *To Change the World: The Irony, Tragedy, and Possibility of Christianity in the Late Modern World* (New York, NY: Oxford University Press Inc., 2010), 277.
18. Keller, *Loving the City*, 125.
19. Keller, *Loving the City*, 122.
20. Ellul, *The Meaning of the City*, 173.
21. Alvin Padilla, "Jesus and the City," Gordon-Conwell Theological Seminary, 2009, https://web.archive.org/web/20180830174500/http://www.gordonconwell.edu/resources/Jesus-and-the-City.cfm.
22. Ellul, *The Meaning of the City*, 121–122.
23. John Inge, *A Christian Theology of Place: Explorations in Practical, Pastoral, and Empirical Theology* (New York: Routledge, 2016), 55.
24. Inge, *A Christian Theology of Place*, 55.
25. Padilla, "Jesus and the City."
26. Harvie M. Conn and Manuel Ortiz, *Urban Ministry: The Kingdom, the City and the People of God* (Downers Grove, IL: InterVarsity Press, 2001), 128.
27. Wayne A. Meeks, *The First Urban Christians: The Social World of the Apostle Paul* (New Haven, CT: Yale University Press, 2003), 8, 11.

28. Keller, *Loving the City*, 131.
29. Roland Allen, *Missionary Methods: St. Paul's or Ours?* (Grand Rapids, MI: Wm. B. Eerdmans Publishing Co., 1962), 17.
30. Gerd Theissen, *The Social Setting of Pauline Christianity: Essays on Corinth* (Eugene, OR: Wipf and Stock Publishers, 2004), 38.
31. Conn and Ortiz, *Urban Ministry*, 140.
32. Lesslie Newbigin, *The Gospel in a Pluralistic Society* (Grand Rapids, MI: Win. B. Eerdmans Publishing Co., 1989), vii.
33. Newbigin, *The Gospel in a Pluralistic Society*, 234.
34. Keller, *Loving the City*, 134.
35. Inge, *A Christian Theology of Place*, 137.
36. Hans Küng, *The Church* (New York, NY: Burns and Oates, 1968).
37. Küng, *The Church*, 274.
38. Tom White, *City-Wide Prayer Movements: One Church, Many Congregations* (Sisters, OR: Servant Publications, 2001), 52.
39. A movement in North America during the early part of the twentieth century that sought to maintain a firm commitment to major "fundamentals" of the Christian faith, especially emphasizing the historical reliability of the supernatural events and affirmations recorded in Scripture (e.g., the virgin birth of Christ, the resurrection of Christ, and the inspiration of Scripture). Fundamentalism was a direct response to the increasing influence of emerging "liberal" forms of Christianity that were growing within Protestant seminaries and churches in the United States.
40. A movement in the late nineteenth and early twentieth centuries in Protestant circles that sought to adapt Christianity to modern thought and culture. Philosophically, liberalism embraced an anti-supernatural approach to Christianity and the Bible. Practically, this resulted in mainly emphasizing social justice over evangelism.
41. This term was originally coined by Harold Ockenga (1947) to describe an uprising in the broader evangelical movement that emphasized engagement with culture and in some cases encouraged cooperation with other more liberally minded Christian groups. Neo-evangelicals were initially concerned with proclaiming both the personal and social dimensions of the Gospel.

42. Derived from the Greek word *euangelion* (i.e., "Gospel," "Good News"), Evangelicals are characterized by emphasizing the need to experience personal conversion through faith in Christ and His death and resurrection. Evangelicals also uphold the inspiration and authority of Scripture as the infallible guide for Christian faith and practice.
43. Carl F. H. Henry, *The Uneasy Conscience of Modern Fundamentalism* (Grand Rapids, MI: Wm. B. Eerdmans Publishing Co., 2003), ix–x.
44. Kenneth S. Kantzer, "The Charismatics among Us," *Christianity Today* 24, no. 4 (February 22, 1980): 25.
45. Bakke, A *Theology as Big as the City*, 19.
46. Clifford Green, ed., *Churches, Cities, and Human Community: Urban Ministry in the United States*, 1945–1985 (Grand Rapids: W. B. Eerdmans, 1996), 48.
47. Those who are engaged in the study of Christian missions.
48. Samuel Escobar, "From Lausanne 1974 to Manilla 1989: The Pilgrimage of Urban Mission," *Urban Mission* 7 no. 4 (1990): 24.
49. Bakke, A *Theology as Big as the City*.
50. Keller, *Center Church*, 24.
51. Leonardo Blair, "Tim Keller Warns Christians About Being Divided by Politics: 'You're Christian First,'" The Christian Post Inc., October 28, 2016, https://www.christianpost.com/news/tim-keller-warns-christians-about-being-divided-by-politics-youre-christian-first-171157/.
52. Bakke, A *Theology as Big as the City*, 21.
53. Eric Swanson and Sam Williams, *To Transform a City: Whole Church, Whole Gospel, Whole City* (Grand Rapids, MI: Zondervan, 2010), 22.
54. "What Is CityServe Portland?," CityServe Portland, https://web.archive.org/web/20190123151828/http://cityservepdx.org/.
55. For more information about City Gospel Movements, visit https://citygospelmovements.org.
56. CityUnite, Vimeo, accessed February 9, 2025, https://vimeo.com/user28964922.
57. "About," Surge Network, accessed March 5, 2021, https://surgenetwork.com/about/.

58. "About," Christ Together Greater Austin, accessed February 9, 2025, https://www.christtogethergreateraustin.com/about/.
59. Church United, Facebook, accessed February 9, 2025, https://www .facebook.com/ChurchUnitedFL/about/.
60. "What Is a City Gospel Movement?" City Gospel Movements, accessed February 9, 2025, https://citygospelmovements.org /trending-questions/#WhatisCGM.
61. Hoskins, "The Identity and Organization of Gospel City Movements in the United States."
62. Hoskins, "The Identity and Organization of Gospel City Movements in the United States."
63. Hoskins, "The Identity and Organization of Gospel City Movements in the United States."
64. Hoskins, "The Identity and Organization of Gospel City Movements in the United States."
65. Hoskins, "The Identity and Organization of Gospel City Movements in the United States."
66. Hoskins, "The Identity and Organization of Gospel City Movements in the United States."
67. Hoskins, "The Identity and Organization of Gospel City Movements in the United States."
68. Hoskins, "The Identity and Organization of Gospel City Movements in the United States."
69. Hoskins, "The Identity and Organization of Gospel City Movements in the United States."
70. Hoskins, "The Identity and Organization of Gospel City Movements in the United States."
71. Hoskins, "The Identity and Organization of Gospel City Movements in the United States."
72. Hoskins, "The Identity and Organization of Gospel City Movements in the United States."
73. Hoskins, "The Identity and Organization of Gospel City Movements in the United States."
74. Hoskins, "The Identity and Organization of Gospel City Movements in the United States."
75. Hoskins, "The Identity and Organization of Gospel City Movements in the United States."

76. Hoskins, "The Identity and Organization of Gospel City Movements in the United States."
77. Hoskins, "The Identity and Organization of Gospel City Movements in the United States."
78. John Kania and Mark Kramer, "Collective Impact," *Stanford Social Innovation Review* 9, no. 1 (Winter 2011): 36–41.
79. Kania and Kramer, "Collective Impact."
80. Norman Walzer, Liz Weaver, and Catherine McGuire eds., "Collective Impact Approaches and Community Development Issues," *Community Development* 47, no. 2 (2016): 156–166.
81. Walzer, Weaver, and McGuire, "Collective Impact Approaches and Community Development Issues," 157.
82. Kania and Kramer, "Collective Impact."
83. Küng, *The Church*, 263.
84. William G. McLoughlin, *Revivals, Awakenings, and Reform* (Chicago, IL: The University of Chicago Press, 1978), x.
85. McLoughlin, *Revivals, Awakenings, and Reform*, 2.